Democracy in Action

Nicolas Brasch

THOMSON
NELSON

Australia · Canada · Mexico · New Zealand · Singapore · Spain · United Kingdom · United States

THOMSON
NELSON

Fast Forward is published by Thomson Learning Australia and distributed as follows:
AUSTRALIA	NEW ZEALAND	CANADA
Level 7, 80 Dorcas Street	Unit 4B, Rosedale Office Park	1120 Birchmount Road
South Melbourne 3205	331 Rosedale Road	Toronto, ON MIK 5G4
Victoria	Albany, North Shore 0632	

First published in 2008
10 9 8 7 6 5 4 3 2 1
11 10 09 08

Text © 2008 Nelson Australia Pty Ltd

Copyright
Apart from fair dealing for the purposes of study, research, criticism or review, or as permitted under Part VB of the Copyright Act, no part of this book may be reproduced by any process without permission. Copyright owners may take legal action against a person who infringes their copyright through unauthorised copying. Enquiries should be directed to the publisher.

Democracy in Action
ISBN-10   0 17 012722 2
ISBN-13   978 0 17 012722 6
ISBN-10   0 17 012717 6 (set)
ISBN-13   978 0 17 012717 2 (set)

Text by Nicolas Brasch
Edited by Cameron Macintosh
Designed by Stella Vassiliou
Series Design by James Lowe
Production Controller Seona Galbally
Photo Research by Michelle Cottrill
Audio recordings by Juliet Hill, Picture Start
Spoken by Matthew King and Abbe Holmes
Printed in China by 1010 Printing International Ltd

This title is published under the imprint of Thomson Nelson.
Nelson Australia Pty Ltd ACN 058 280 149 (incorporated in Victoria) trading as Thomson Learning Australia.

Email nelson@thomsonlearning.com.au
Website www.thomsonlearning.com.au

Acknowledgements
The author and publisher would like to acknowledge permission to reproduce material from the following sources:
Photographs by AAP Image, p. 9/ AFP, p. 16/ AFP/ Greenpeace, front cover top, pp. 1 top, 8/ Alan Porritt, pp. 3, 5, 10, 23/ Luis Ascui, p. 22/ Mark Baker, p. 11/ Stringer, p. 7; Fairfax Photos/ Chris Lane, p. 21; Istockphoto/ Zdenka Micka, p. 12; Newspix/ Chris Hyde, p. 18/ Kym Smith, p. 4; Photodisc, front cover bottom, p. 1 bottom; Photolibrary/ David Burnett, p. 6/ Grant Frank, p. 17/ Marc Romanelli, p. 15/ Photoresearchers, back cover, p. 20; Stockbyte, p. 19.

THE UNIVERSITY OF MELBOURNE

Evaluated in independent research by staff from the Department of Language, Literacy and Arts Education at the University of Melbourne.

Democracy in Action

Nicolas Brasch

Contents

Chapter 1	**Making Decisions**	4
Chapter 2	**Floating the Issue**	8
Chapter 3	**Writing Letters**	12
Chapter 4	**Lobbying and Pressure**	16
Chapter 5	**Polls and Protests**	20
Glossary and Index		24

Chapter 1

MAKING DECISIONS

Every day, in every country around the world, governments make decisions. The decision-making process can take a long time in countries with a **democratic system** of government. This is because many different people want to have their say – they want to take part in the democratic process.

members of the Australian parliament vote on new laws

a meeting between US and Australian government representatives

There are many ways in which people take part in the democratic process. We can clearly see this process in action by looking at one issue – nuclear energy.

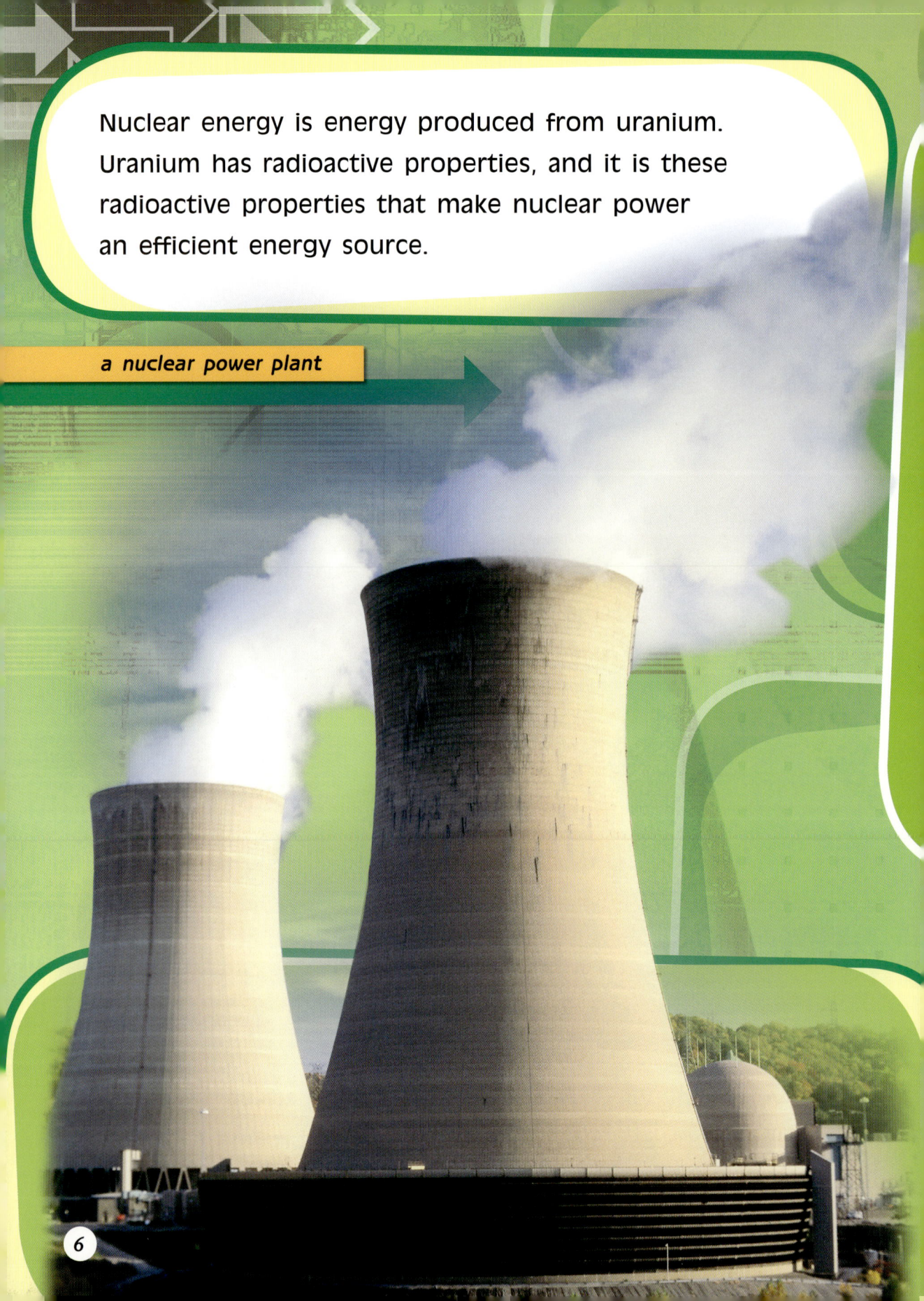

Nuclear energy is energy produced from uranium. Uranium has radioactive properties, and it is these radioactive properties that make nuclear power an efficient energy source.

a nuclear power plant

radioactive waste

However, the production of nuclear energy also produces radioactive waste that can be very harmful to humans. Also, when uranium is **enriched**, it can be used to make nuclear weapons. For these reasons, the introduction of nuclear energy is an issue that some people would support and others would oppose.

Chapter 2
FLOATING THE ISSUE

An issue such as nuclear energy is **controversial**. A government considering the introduction of nuclear energy would know that some people would oppose it and others would support it. Governments do not want to put too many people 'off side' because they want to be re-elected at the next election.

an anti-nuclear protest

Running Words 200

a public debate

So, a government proposing to introduce nuclear energy would want to get a debate started in the community that would give it an idea about how the people feel about this issue. This is sometimes called 'floating an issue'.

The most common way for a government to 'float an issue' is to use the media. Politicians and the media need each other. The media needs politicians because the public wants to read and hear about major political stories. Politicians need the media so that their views can be heard by the public.

A government proposing to introduce nuclear energy could ask one of its politicians to make a speech about nuclear energy. Or, the politician might give a journalist a personal interview. This would usually be enough to get the issue into the media and into the **public domain**.

Chapter 3

WRITING LETTERS

Once the issue has been brought into the public domain, anyone can have their say. In a democratic society, there are many different ways in which people can have their say on an issue. One way is to write a letter or an email to a newspaper or to a politician.

LETTERS TO THE EDITOR

Dear Editor,

At last the issue of nuclear energy is being discussed. For too long, the opponents of this efficient form of energy have dominated discussions. But the fact is that nuclear energy produces far less pollution than coal and gas. In other words, it is better for the environment. Let's now have a discussion about nuclear energy instead of the one-sided debate that has gone on so far.

Bill Young, Fairfield

The Daily Times

To: info@government.com.au
Cc:
Subject: Nuclear energy debate

Dear Ms Best,

As you are my representative in parliament (and someone I voted for), I want you to know how I feel about the current debate about nuclear energy.

Nuclear energy should never, ever be considered in this country. It doesn't matter how safe a nuclear power plant is – even one accident at such a plant could kill thousands of people through the spread of radiation. Also, if we create a nuclear industry in this country, we can't be sure that some of the enriched uranium won't be used to create a nuclear bomb.

Instead of thinking about nuclear energy, the government should be looking at investing in alternative forms of energy, such as wind and solar power.

I hope you will consider my views, and those of many others who share such views, when deciding which way you will vote on the issue of nuclear energy.

Meredith Green

15

Chapter 4

LOBBYING AND PRESSURE

It's not just individuals who have their say in a democratic society. Companies and organisations also make sure that their views are heard.

In the case of nuclear energy, the types of companies and organisations that would want to convince the government to introduce nuclear energy include uranium mining companies and companies that produce equipment and technology for the nuclear industry.

a uranium mine in Australia's Northern Territory

an open pit coal mine

The types of companies and organisations that would want to convince the government not to introduce nuclear energy include environmental groups and coal mining companies who would see nuclear energy as a threat to their business.

There are two major ways that companies and large organisations try to sway politicians to their points of view: lobbying and pressure.

Lobbying involves speaking to politicians or their advisors. Sometimes, high-level members of a company or organisation are powerful enough to make an appointment with a politician. But many companies and organisations use lobbyists. Lobbyists are people with political connections. They might be ex-politicians or ex-political advisers who are well known to the current politicians.

Companies and organisations can also put pressure on politicians, in a number of ways. They can threaten to take their business to other countries. They can speak to the media, and they can stop giving money to political parties.

Chapter 5

POLLS AND PROTESTS

Two other ways in which people have their say in a democratic society are through opinion polls and protests.

Political opinion polls are surveys of how people feel about an issue or political party. A polling company will ask members of the public a number of questions.

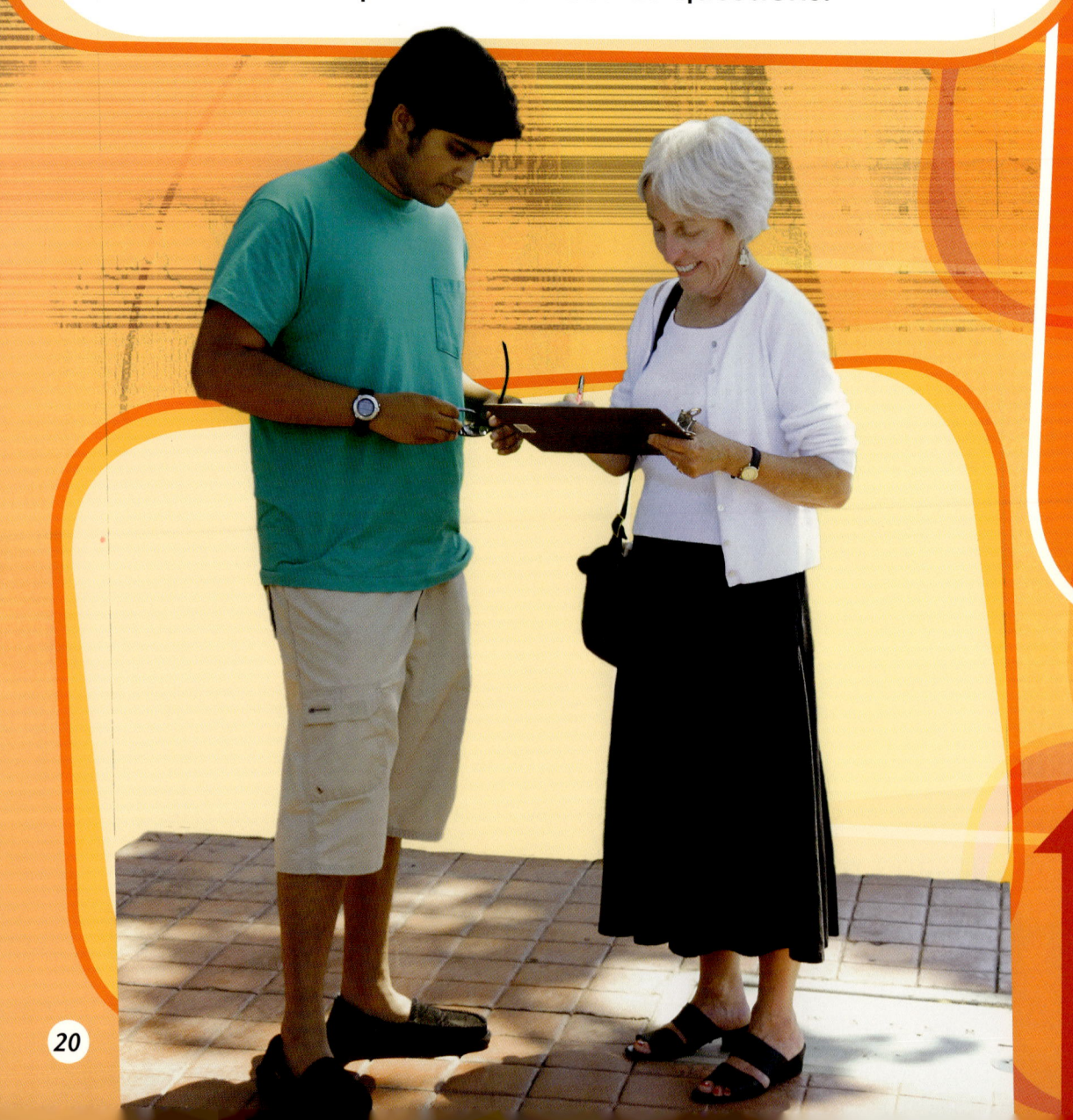

Politicians will study the results of the survey and may even change their **policies** because of the results.

A protest is a gathering of people who oppose a policy or course of action. Politicians will not change their minds because of a small protest, but if thousands of people take part in a public protest, a political party may change its mind on an issue. An issue as controversial as the introduction of nuclear energy would be likely to lead to large protests.

Once all the debate and discussion is over, and the lobbyists have finished their meetings, and the protesters have packed up their placards and gone home, the government has to decide whether or not it wants to go ahead with a policy.

That's democracy in action.

Glossary

controversial	something that causes strong differences of opinion
democratic system	a system of government in which the citizens of a country elect their leaders
enriched	changed into a form that can be used to generate nuclear power
policies	ideas about how things should be done
public domain	able to be accessed by the public

Index

companies   16, 17, 18, 19

debate   9, 13, 14, 23

democratic process   4–5

floating an issue   8–11

government   4, 8, 9, 10, 11, 14, 16, 17, 23

letter writing   12–14

lobbying   18

media   10–11, 19

nuclear energy   5, 6–7, 8, 9, 11, 13, 14, 16, 17, 22

organisations   16, 17, 18, 19

politicians   10, 11, 12, 18, 19, 21, 22

polls   20–21

pressure   18, 19

protests   20, 22

public domain   11, 12

uranium   6, 7, 14, 16